POST-DIAGNOSIS

Post-Diagnosis

Sandra Steingraber

Firebrand
Books

Portions of this work (often in different versions or with different titles) have appeared in the following publications: *Benchmark: Anthology of Contemporary Illinois Poetry* (Stormline Press), *Blue Ox Review, Columbia Poetry Review, Denver Quarterly, Great River Review, Hiram Poetry Review, Michigan Quarterly Review, One in Three: Women With Cancer Confront an Epidemic* (Cleis Press), *Radcliffe Quarterly, Spoon River Quarterly,* and *Triquarterly.*

Book design by Nightwood Design
Cover design by Debra Engstrom
Cover art by Nancy Spero

Printed in the United States on acid-free paper by McNaughton & Gunn

10 9 8 7 6 5 4 3 2 1

Library of Congress Cataloging-in-Publication Data

Steingraber, Sandra.
    Post-diagnosis / by Sandra Steingraber.
        p.   cm.
    ISBN 1-56341-057-5 (pbk.) —ISBN 1-56341-058-3 (cloth)
    1.Cancer—Patients—United States—Poetry. 2. Women—United States—Poetry.
I. Title.
PS3569.T377P67   1995
811'.54—dc20   94-49696
                                                                      CIP

Acknowledgments

I wish to thank Karol Bennett, Judith Brady, Brian Burt, Valerie Cornell, Robert Currie, Denise Dilnot, Carolyn Forché, Lucia Getsi, Lawrence Goldstein, Kimberly McCarthy, John McDonald, James McGowan, Karen Lee Osborne, Alicia Ostriker, Linda Pastan, Charlotte Sheedy, Shane Snowdon, Keith Taylor, and Rachel Guido deVries for their suggestions and close readings of these poems. Thanks are also due my editor Nancy K. Bereano of Firebrand Books, the Women's Community Cancer Project of Cambridge, and Florence Ladd for saying, "You will."

I am grateful to the Ragdale Foundation and to the Bunting Institute of Radcliffe College for the residencies and financial support that made this book possible. Also to the Money for Women/ Barbara Deming Memorial Fund for a writing grant.

for the nonsurvivors

Contents

Stories from Memory

The Living and the Dead

Notes

In Response to a Promotional Ad Claiming That the Number of People Who Have Survived Cancer Could Now Fill the City of Los Angeles

And the nonsurvivors fill the Pacific Ocean,
the Grand Canyon, and the whole of Antarctica.
They fill our silences. And they fill our mouths
when we try to speak. They inhabit vast and
magnificent cities. The nonsurvivors remember
Los Angeles as just a dot on the map—a stone's
throw in the sticks where everybody knew each
other's business. And then there is the wife
of the man in Illinois: he's been walking
the streets for thirty years because the space
of her body fills every living room of every house
he sees.

Walk along the banks of the Grand Calumet, walk
to Ground Zero, Nevada, go down to Oak Ridge,
Tennessee. Point out to folks that no one can sleep
in Los Angeles: the breastless, hairless ones always
scratching at the city walls, howling at the gates
all night. Everybody wants to be an angel.

The dead are smaller than us. We have to remember
that. The dead take up so little room. Their
houses are modest, they drive small cars.
They've stopped dreaming of going West.

11

You called this morning to say a new tumor had
flowered in your liver and another in a small coil
of the intestine. I murmured something, promised
to make a few phone calls. I hardly know you
actually. But I had mentioned once that I was a
resident of that lucky city. Sweet California.

COUNTING BACKWARD

WAITING FOR THE LAB REPORTS, THINKING OF PENELOPE

Outside it stops raining.
I weave and unweave the ribbons
of my nightgown. A nurse
presents breakfast and leaves.
My mother comes to braid
my neglected hair.
The activities therapist
brings yarn and a needlepoint canvas:
a stiff red cardinal in a tree branch.
Someone who has been crying all night
is still crying.
Outside it starts to rain.

I must have been fourteen when
I first learned how Odysseus' wife
bought time. Unweaving:
the widening part in a woman's hair.
Chemotherapy: and the whole dark
tapestry unravels, the bird's
black feet unthread the black branch
and fly away.

Penelope, did you see them
in the operating room—
their blue masks, gathering closer,
our suitors, their urgency?

BONE SCAN

You submit by making a fist.
This is where the long process of unlikelihood
begins.

I make mine by curling the thumb
over top of the knuckles
the way the boy in homeroom showed me
the year the bus stop threats flew so thick
my eyes blurred with fear.

The way they are now.
The way yours will be.

"Not the sissy way," he reproached,
pulling my thumb from its foolish
grip inside the four other fingers.
"You'll break a bone that way
swinging it into the bitch's face."

You begin with a fist
and then you lay the throbbing arm down
so the blue vein can rise to meet
the probing rubbery fingers.
This is how you submit
to the lead canister decaled
with red and yellow atomic flowers
as it opens now like an Easter egg.
And nested inside: the syringe.

Make a fist, please. And release.
And make a fist. And release.

There are other lessons to unlearn.
Water, for example, serves to concentrate,
speeding the isotope's uptake
into the cells of the skeleton you hadn't known
could be a sponge for such poison.
You can go where you like for this part—
back to the waiting room or to lunch
still being served in the cafeteria.
Two quarts in two hours is recommended.

Now you yourself are the X-ray,
both photographer and landscape, exposed
and exposing, your whole radioactive self
positioned under the black absorbing plates.
Teeth, ribs, sockets, the spine's
bony rope, any hard place an errant
cancer cell could latch on, wrap around,
suck onto like a barnacle on a ship's hull:
the image of your Halloween body rises
slowly into the color monitor.

Know that the unholy energy streaming
out of your bones has nothing at all
to do with you, gripped as you are
in a half-life of absolute motionlessness,
obediently breathing as lightly as possible.
Just as the pianist knows nothing
about what the page turner is thinking
during the whole long solo.

You can pass the time with meditation,
visualization. You can hope
what you want to hope.
By predetermination, someone
in the technical audience will be cruel,
talking petulantly and ceaselessly
above your head to somebody else.
She doesn't care about you.
Here is a trick: send your soul out
into the straight bones of your fingers
as they lie there, emitting and emitting.
Imagine them curling, thumb on the outside.
Imagine the fist as it comes crashing
into those teeth.

SCHEDULED SURGERY

And she is one
and she is the other one

                                    in a nearby room

who made an angel to stand guard
as she counted backward

                            someone is giving instructions

into the dark grip of anesthesia

                            I can't quite make out   *sandra*
                                count for us sandra can you
                                        count for us?

as her body blurred and opened
she flew herself over to the angel

and commanded it: *watch*
                                        watch over me
                                        watch watch
                                        watch over me

LETTER TO THE CITY

for William Allen

...among the deer...in both solitary and more social species the two sexes operate almost completely independently of each other. While sexual separation among solitary animals is perhaps not surprising, even among the more social species the sexes remain separate for most of the year and come together only during the short breeding season to mate.
The Natural History of Deer

Therefore, I say, the museum dioramas lie.
But you say no, that you've
seen deer families just like that—
gathered in the tiny cemetery
you and I strayed into once—
all three of them among the stones:
buck, doe, and fawn,
their mouths working the hard
little apples the wind brings them
full of rot and wine.

Tonight I believe you, Bill,

for what do I know?
While your mother was pelting
your father's car with rocks
I was crouched at the edge
of a field, vowing never to go home.

Sometimes it's impossible to tell
the truth. The day my grandfather
died I inked a little trail
of teardrops into my blue diary
but did not cry—a posture of grief
I would learn to perfect.

20

But I wanted it to be true!
Just as I had wanted him to say to me,
You've got your mother's eyes.

So when you first showed me the stone
you found, etched with three mysterious lines,
I missed the significance.
I wanted the pattern to be something
of the stone itself alone—
marks left by an ancient sea or the body
of a dying leaf or anything
sorrowful or lost—
and thought the evidence that someone's
knife had scraped them there
made it counterfeit.

I was wrong. But I have carried this stone
with me since the night your hand
pressed its weight into mine.
Now, posed in a diorama of my own,
I, too, can see the three of them together
in the stone: father, mother, fawn.

Yet this is also true:
if we watched them long enough
we would see the buck become tormented
and leave the miniature scene,
the windfall apples—the bloody skin
around his antlers throbbing.
Alone, his throat swells, his head lowers
to spar with branches. I have seen
the strips of velvet, the scrapings
left deep in the bark of trees
by the polished rack of bone.

Field biology has little to say
about the females, who are presumed
to travel in doe groups
or with their yearling sons.
So all I can tell you is this:

Bill, sometimes I am as frightened
as a buck whose antlers are locked
around the branches of a sapling pine
and the wind is blowing.

POST-OP, JANUARY ICE STORM

There is this burden

> *as in winter when rain*
> *falls and freezes*
> *the weight of water*
> *twisting cedars*
> *to the ground*

A kind of great difficulty

> *when to move*
> *means to break apart*
> *like a cedar sheeted in ice*
> *when the wind*
> *begins*

Or maybe it is just
the uselessness of splendor

> *in the window sunlight*
> *shimmering in the cedars*
> *waxwings blinking*
> *by the glass berries*

How Are You? Are You Fine?

Some mornings I wake up
and discover my body
is a soft cloth bag.
Bright acrylic plush
on the outside, scratchy
mesh on the inside.

Sometime during the night
my eyes bugged out
into two scuffed domes
with black disks
that loll about.

Paste sutures my skull
together. There is
a hand in my head.
When the hand clenches
I scowl and everyone
claps.

The hand
in my head is mine.

A thumb pushes up under
the felt strip of
my tongue. *Yes,*
says the puppeteer,
using my voice,
I am fine!

COLLABORATIONISTS

God and I haven't spoken for years.
Neither of us can remember what
the original argument was about.
I am not going to be the one
to apologize, I shout.

The angels confer, offer
to smooth things over for me.
Like mothers they want peace.
Like mothers they don't tell
the whole story.

History of Atomic Bomb Testing: A Memory Exercise

You wake up in the morning with a dream. You begin with writing down the last scene, and you write your way back to the beginning.
A Little Course in Dreams

ZEBRA. YOKE. X-RAY. WILLIAM.
Here I am waking up in the recovery room.
My uncles troop in, dragging their parachutes.
Where is my father? An argument breaks out.
He reenlisted, he was lost in Italy,
he is a POW, he was sent to the Pacific.
I cry and tear my gown, crusted with sutures
and pearls. It is 1982, my wedding day.
Here I am serving cake on the lawn.
In the oily coolness of the garage
my uncles drink homemade wine and tell
war stories. They are the bricklayers
who built this house for Willie
and his new bride, my mother.
And here she is: standing radiant
among them in her lipstick
and borrowed wedding gown. It is 1952.
VICTOR. UNCLE. TARE. SUGAR.

ROGER. QUEEN. PETER. OBOE.
I am dreaming my way back to How Hour.
Back through Sidewinder, Redwing, and Sandstone.
Back through Schooner, Buggy, and Sulky.
Back through Teapot, Upshot, Bravo,
Hardtack, Wigwam, Yucca, and Swordfish.

Here I am taking off my nightclothes
in front of a mirror. My underpants
are named for an island in the Pacific,
an historical curiosity about which
there are competing schools of thought.
Some say it is because they are tiny:
like an atom. Others say it is because
they reveal the middle of a woman's torso,
which is erotic: like an atom bomb.
Others say it is because the island itself
is missing its middle: vaporized
after detonation. It is 1948.
NAN. MIKE. LOVE. KING.

JIG. ITEM. HOW. GEORGE.
I am dreaming my way back to Zeropoint,
back to Crossroads, back to Bikini.
Here are the ships lying in their sleeping place.
Here are the ruins of bunkers, causeways,
camera mounts. Here are the crypts
of poisoned soil, the graveyard of coconuts.
Here are the electrical cables
welded to coral. It is 1946
on the morning of the waking day.
The ghost fleet rises from the lagoon.
Forty-two thousand men are recalled to the decks
and ordered to watch with their eyes closed.
They see red light and then the bones
of their hands through their eyelids.
Where is my father? Here I am asleep
having a dream. Here is the dream.
FOX. EASY. DOG. CHARLIE.
BAKER. ABLE. ZERO. ONE.

Stage Directions for a Homecoming

AT RISE:
Living room
interior
of an apartment.
Modest.
Furniture is nice
but does not match
as though
gathered over time
from second
hand shops.

A fondness for oak.

Room should be
decorated to show
it is the home
of a woman
who lives alone.
For example

the windows
may be covered with
Scottish lace curtains but
there are no pictures
on the walls or

the walls
are hung with elegant
and well-framed art but
the windows
are bare.

Soft ambient light.

At left is a door
and a wooden coat rack.
One wool coat
and scarf hang
on the hook.
There is snow
on the scarf.

On the floor
next to the coat
a small suitcase.

At stage right
a comfortable chair
upholstered
in a pleasing color.
Next to the chair
is a table of the type
that men use
to lay their keys
and spare change on
before undressing.

Two books are
on the table.
One is full of words
like Triumph
Odyssey Courage Struggle.
It is the author's
Personal Story.
The other book
is entitled
Departure.

THE CHARACTER:
is sprawled on the chair
taking up space.
One leg is outstretched.
Both arms rest
on the armrests.
She should be
wearing something
odd. An outfit
someone chose for her
or something she herself
pulled from the closet
just before leaving
for the hospital.

Downstage
a dog sleeps
in such total relief
that its legs
twitch.

Someone has remembered
to water the plants.

A brief tableau.

TIME:
The present.

(This scene can be repeated indefinitely. Chance of death
rises with frequency of homecoming.)

Post-Diagnosis

I'm not trying to say it's not
a good place. It is—
this house where I eat and breathe
and stomp off the cold.
The afternoon sun slants through
a prism I hung on the curtain rod,
scattering clean colors.
I scrub the stout-legged bathtub
to squeakiness, unload
the heavy sacks of groceries.
My green-fibered plants grow
succulent on their window ledges.
I do too.

But sometimes late at night
I notice sounds through my books,
the scruffling of feet
in the walls. I strain to hear
the twitching whiskers....
My lover laughs. "Those are pigeons,
San, not rats in the roof."
I dumbly nod and go to bed,
go to warm arms, but protected
against, fearing
the contamination of sperm.

I'm not trying to say it's not
a good place but years later
and still I fear infestation—
staring at specks of dust
that flicker in a spot of sun,

shuddering to think what we breathe
into our spongy lungs.
This is absurd, I know.
I look up the word Remission
("release, as from a debt;
restored, put back")
and in the kitchen I pour
macaroni into boiling water.
Tiny beetles spill out
with the noodles, swirl in the pan,
belly up, legs curled.

Look, that meant nothing.
I am restored, put back.
I am not like those others,
full of metastases, who are returned
to their lives as guests,
who have only a journey,
who are packing their bags,
who are leaving now.
A week ago my surgeon rose
from his instruments and laughed.
"Sandra, let's grow old together."
The tests were negative. He is young man
and I told him this was a good place,
a good place to live.

But sometimes late at night
I still see the lights of the hospital—
the white hushed comings and goings,
the gray partitioning curtains,
the slow dripping in tubes.
Outside this window the last
summer flowers hemorrhage
in the garden and winter lies
like a tumor beneath the earth.

WATCH

PREFATORY

I am often unsure
how   to begin

as a bird who
holds in her mouth
the first twigs
of a new nest

and not far below
the gray cat
squinting
in the full sun

Research Notes

1.

In the laboratory, a dog shocked by electrical currents will learn to jump a simple barrier to escape pain. If two dogs, A and B, are yoked together such that both receive shocks but only dog A is able to jump, then dog A will learn to leap the barrier and save both animals from pain. If, however, dogs A and B are subsequently unyoked, dog A will continue to jump while dog B will lie passively even when the current is high, the pain level intense, and the barrier to escape low. Dog B has been conditioned to the prior reality that only the actions of another can stop pain.

This is called Learned Helplessness.

2.

The patient was positioned, prepped, and draped in the usual fashion. *A solitary papillary frond, grade I carcinoma, appears on slide 2. We do not see its attachment.* A 15.5 cystourethroscope was inserted into the bladder. *With the specimen in fixative the papillary fronds are seen to freely wave. The tumor as a whole, grade II carcinoma, resembles a spider or a potted fern plant.* The patient tolerated the procedure and left the O.R. in satisfactory condition. *The subsequent stroma shows no evidence of invasion. The mucus layer is soft pink in color.* Physical examination revealed a very pleasant, slender, tall 24-year-old white female. Her neck had no adenopathy. The lungs were clear. Both breasts, although very small, revealed no abnormalities.

3.

Infants are born knowing how to make a fist. It is innate. Stimulated by a twig, a finger, or a strand of hair, a newborn's fingers clench instinctively. First the third finger bends, then fingers two, four, and five. The thumb is last. This response has been observed in fetuses 65 millimeters long. First the third finger bends, then fingers two, four, and five.

This is called the Palmar Reflex.

Apology to Audre Lorde,
Never Sent

Years later, she came to my university to speak. She said all the beautiful things: about the master's tools and the master's house, about learning to speak when we are afraid. In the back of the auditorium, I wanted my brain to be a tape recorder, a programmed VCR. I wanted my head to be a magnetic tape so that my soul could fly out to where it was already flying, flying to the space with no name, the space that is absence, the space where the cloth folds along her chest, the phantom, amputated space, smooth and broad, a site of violence that she will not hide or reconstruct. I wanted to fall into that emptiness. I was falling, like into tall grass that has grown over war and is peace. I was falling, as though to lie and sleep, curled along her scar like a river.

Please, do not romanticize this. Surely, this is pornography. Come back, my soul, you cannot go there.

Oh, Audre, I heard you've had news of a recent metastasis. I want to tell you about my mother's paper towel breasts, how they felt against my ribs when she embraced me. Paper towels, like she's trying to mop up a little accident. Soak up spilled milk she won't cry over, she says, handing me her copies of Norman Vincent Peale, Helen Steiner Rice, all her three-named authors whose books I broke windows with. Anger purifies. Audre, I want to tell you about the catheter tube that stretched between my own two legs, how I still reach for it in my sleep, that horrible penis. Your words saved me. I was yoked to terrible things then. So, during the questions and answers, I did stand up in that auditorium, shaking like I am now, to say thank you. To say that I had jumped the barrier myself and was saved now. Afterward, in the wine and cheese room, I was embarrassed, I averted my gaze. And then someone nudged me, whispered, "She wants you." And unbelievingly I looked and saw her smiling and beckoning to me as though from a distant shore, motioning me to sit down beside her. And I began swimming against an immense current, passing the long snake of people queued before her for book signing.

Oh, Audre. My mother's paper towel breasts pressing my own. It hurt so much. And then me, and everyone thinking it's genetic, but it's not, you know. I was an adopted child, another story, not mine, unremembered, before language. But I memorized your words: "The idea that happiness can insulate us against the results of our environmental madness is a rumor circulated by our enemies to destroy us." The world's largest trash incinerator is going on line in Detroit, and by their own admission, it will raise the cancer rate here. Who speaks for the air and the water? I want to. Oh, Audre, let's leave this hall and walk to the hospital together. We can stroll along the Huron River and look up at its bank of lights in the darkness. We can walk toward the red glow that spells out the word EMERGENCY above a lighted arrow, a direction only last month I walked myself. And as we move through that space, I'll ask you how it is that on the sixth floor cancer ward women wake through Demerol and beg to live, and three flights up in the psychiatric ward they sink into Xanax and beg to die. Are there two hells for women, each distinct?

39

God, what am I doing? I sound like the women in the audience of my own poetry readings. The ones who think they know me, who slip me notes and telephone numbers, who afterward have to tell me about their own diagnoses and breakdowns and ask what they should do. The benefit reading for the women's crisis center was the worst. How I just wanted to scream, "Get away, it's just poetry, how do you know what I say is about me? I have a Ph.D. and a good prognosis. I don't live there anymore." Don't you hate reverence, Audre? All that worship of blood, and moon, and soil?

In truth, I said nothing. I said none of this as I swam the current of awkwardness toward her. I sat on the shoreline, wild and half-drowned, brimming with confession, saying nothing. I remember she held my hand between both of hers. She asked me, "Have I given you everything you need from me tonight?" And, still disbelieving, I shook my head. Finally, I said, "Yes, oh, yes, yes, yes." And she answered, "Your mouth is saying yes, but your head is saying no. What do you mean?"

CUSTODY

First woman: Death is there; death is here.
              But you are both blind and deaf.
Jason: But—the—children are well?

Medea

Tonight the ward is quiet. And the nurses merciful. Hours
they have let us two sit in the beige dayroom's half-light
and for once do not harry us off to bed with their jangle
of keys, flashlights angling down the corridor.

I refuse sleep—that room of dreams I'm nightly dragged
off to and forced to watch some treacherous plot unfold
in which someone's always walking away and I'm left beg-
ging. And you, Darlene, swaying on the sofa like a moon
full of tears, sad planet, you never sleep. Prescription junkie,
the meds withdrawing and you've been begging all day.
Now they've equipped you with a regulation Walkman
and let you wait the night out here, singing and rocking
in the cradle of your own round flesh.

Darlene, I know you're here because you tried to kill your
children. Now the courts have stripped you of all custody
and packed the children off to live with their father, a
man who despises you. I've seen the photos on your bed-
side table. Two boys—they are so small—their eyes soft
like yours.

Now you're somewhere else, alone with your little radio,
singing in that quavering, tuneless way:

I celebrate my love for you...mmm-hhhmm
I wanna get close to you...beside me...
mmm-mmm-hhmm...hold me and guide me...

41

It's so quiet tonight, Darlene. In my room, Tina sleeps the fast-pulsed sleep of an anorexic, curled like a bony violin, towels pressed between her knees to prevent bruising. I asked her how it felt to be so thin. "It hurts," she said.

Darlene, when I think of you back in that kitchen—the knife raised, the two little ones skittering across the floor, the chairs all crashing, the capsules rolling into the sink, all the mouths rounded into no no no—I think of Euripides' Medea. Medea herself when she looks into the children's eyes and sees defilement: the fruits of a past she wants only to annihilate. How else to show the traitor Jason that loathing him is endless? And anyway, wasn't he already on his way, sword drawn, with all the might of Corinth, and intent to harm?

And anyway, didn't the man hold your own head up to that same kitchen wall night after night, Darlene, and say, "Bitch, I'm going to fucking kill you?"

Darlene, these last few months I've lost custody of a lot. But I think we could redo this myth. "Better to be clean bones on the shore," Medea cried before the knife came down. "Bones have no eyes to weep." But suppose, when she looked into the children's faces, she saw not Jason's but her own intelligent eyes. Suppose they were daughters. Suppose she stayed her hand. Jason would kill her anyway, no matter what she begged, and deliver the children into the hands of strangers. He was always a worm.

But, Darlene, suppose *we* were those children, two girls given over to these custodians. Spared from death, wouldn't we learn to live? The night is long and there is much to reconsider. Sister, keep singing.

WATER OVER ROAD

1.
We only asked where the trail began
and the ranger equipped us
with maps, warnings, geological surveys.

It's like that, isn't it?
The path through the woods
curves into a wilder territory
than one imagined standing
at the sunlit edge looking in.
And there's always that decision to make
at the place where the road
lowers into water.

2.
Boundaries, the social workers said
to me before I left the hospital
with my suitcase and walked home
through the obliterating snow.
Okay, I said: There is the river
that drowns everything.
Its course can be charted.
I'll admit there are borders here
somewhere. I need to know
the names of those trees.

3.
You are another country.
Let me touch you again—
What is the name of this road?
Which way are these rivers flowing?

DEER

1.

All summer their accidental slaughter—
a deer drifts from the dark
safety of trees and takes
its place on the road's edge.
Caught between the beams
of moonlight and headlight
it is already dead.
Behind the wheel the driver
dozes or wonders if it will storm.
There is so much grace
in the calm regard
of the illuminated eyes...
but now there will only be
the carnage to contend with
and the tedious inspection of damage.

Suddenly they see each other.

2.

During the thick of winter
they crowd into the last stands
of hemlock and paw the empty ground,
farm dogs tearing at their flanks.
They'll stay there, hunched
in their hunger, until death
or April saves them.
One dark day we watched
a man carry them grain and alfalfa,
branches from his own trees.
They would not eat.

44

When a fluke storm covered
the forest in ice that spring
I thought of the deer,
the birthing does,
and cursed them.

3.

All summer we watched deer
arc through the green trees
and felt we had been blessed.
You showed me their signs:
the torn edges of branches
they had tasted, the flattened
grasses showing where they slept.
At night we flushed them sometimes
by accident from the dark places,
their bodies ghostly as moonbeams.
Years later, my thoughts drift
toward you like salt-hungry deer
to the February highway.

4.

No. Do not say that we
are like them. Say
there are miles of road
between us, lined with
the crumpled bodies of deer.
Say that we must be careful,
my friend, the woods are thick
with deer, their eyes
shining with accusations.

Waiting Room

Seeing large men weeping
disturbs me the way
pictures of this planet
taken from the moon do.
I mean the ones that show
the globe all blue and quivering
in its filmy skin of atmosphere.

I mean the sight of
the robust physician
sobbing   *my god my god*
into a telephone
when I stumbled into
the wrong waiting room.

I mean last night, your shoulders
trembling in the doorway
the moon following the path
your tears made down
the skin of your hands.

THIRD PERSON

1.
Always I will see you in your dream,
spilling milk on a cafe table—
only a small casualty
but your lover is so ashamed.
Somewhere the voice of a third person
says your name.

2.
After making love, he used to say,
You are elegant as wheat.
The night I left he dreamed
of walking toward a field
of black grain, of finding
the slender stalks rotted
by insects. I was gone.
There would be someone else.
Emily, why can't we shed our shame
like ugly dresses we're tired
of wearing?

3.
This grief: unendurable but real.
Unlike the dream I have where
someone I love has stopped saying my name.
On those nights I turn to thorns,
banished to a place full of cactus.

We all stand silent in the desert
like tuning forks, listening
for the voice of a third person
who can save us.

4.
Panic flows in our lives, Emily, a river
of milk. Once, out of love, someone
brought me tea when I was sick
and I spilled it, scalding,
over my arm. A small casualty.
That was the night I said,
Please be careful with me,
a phrase I usually only use
with anesthesiologists.

5.
The day after I came home we awoke
to sirens. The landlady's barn
was burning down and she was
beside herself: a small untended fire
spilled out of control. The neighbors
came to watch the streams
of water turn to ice—long thorns
on the blackened rafters, beyond saving.
No one knew each other's name.
I remember how the chickens fled
the smoking henhouse, the red
fleshy flames bobbing in a panic
on their heads. We stayed
until her brother drove in
from town to chastise her carelessness.

Even then I didn't want to leave.
I wanted to write the story
of all of our lives
in the voice of a third person.

SUBLET

Out here in winter
deer print the roads

with their silence
and dark mornings I learn

patience behind schoolbuses
grinding the route into town.

Someone else failed to bring
a living from these eighty acres

of bad drainage. The landlord
can't recollect them anymore,

the mailbox greeting too faded
to spell out their names

though I keep trying.
I know it gets to you sometimes—

the sky's uncertainty,
the misery of chickens.

Under the snow the corn
rots. Some nights

I dream you leave
on imaginary errands

and drive into the city's
lights, into those old

neighborhoods that yield
all their secrets:

Caution   Hidden Drive
Deaf Child at Play

Dominion of Geese

They come out of the lake at dusk
to reclaim the beach from the bathers
and to compose themselves in the wet sand.
They do not speak, nor does the moon
who broods at the water's edge.
Only in the deep trees the whip-poor-will
still pities himself.

Their bodies are like vessels fashioned
from clay by the hands of young girls,
but they will not be bothered
by our admiration, nor by Mars,
jealous planet, who comes now into our sky
dark and furious.

STORIES FROM MEMORY

. . . a knowledge of brief truancy into the sources of my life, whereto I have no rightful access, having paid no price beyond love and sorrow.

JAMES AGEE

I. Mimicry

Once I asked her why she never told us.
She said, *I was like that bird*
that feigns a broken wing to distract
the bad ones from the nest.

Killdeer, a bird that says its name.
Charadrius vociferus, a common plover
found in open fields and pastures
often far from water. I can't say

I fully understand this simile.
Her injury was real. In the photograph
she smiles from underneath a wig
several shades too black, face puffed

from radiation, the rest of her
scooped out. See how her shoulder falls?
My sister says this was the year that all
the doors closed in the house. Before,

on Sundays, we sat in netted skirts
and leotards and watched her dress for church.
Avon bottles, stockings, garter belt and slips.
Her breasts were like twin pears.

After the mastectomy, the bedroom door
stayed shut. I remember none of this.
I collected stamps that year. I prayed to God
to give me breasts and then became

an atheist. You want the written text?
Downstairs in the sewing room, read
the trace of penciled lines behind the door,
with dates that document her secret

rehabilitation as she dragged her arm
a little further up the wall each day.
Now look how this pattern draws the eye
away from the nest of other lines below—

each traced from a ruler laid across
a daughter's head, inscribed with names
and dates to show how big we grew.
Still, she should have told us.

II. Grandparents

And what do we remember after all?
Of him: a black coat, a smelly bathroom.
And at that other house: a large dress
advancing toward us offering bits of gum.

Maybe the smell of matches but more
the taste of flat Coke in glasses without ice.
We were one of so many birthdays they
could never remember. They were nobody's parents

to us, so young we were afraid
of standing near them in the photograph
our parents wanted because they thought
that it might be the last one

and finally it was. Their cats were lame
and mean and our parents cruel to us
inside those houses, where anything
could break, dissolving into reprimands

and tears. They would die. My sister
so young she thought her birthday would never
come again. A black coat, a smelly bathroom.
What else? A dish of old hard candies.

III. Twin Memories

In Michigan a man came home to his
house on a quiet street and found
his son and young wife murdered.
This is not my story to tell.

But I was on the bus that hit a girl
in Mainz. She fled into the traffic
like an animal, holding out her arm.
I know the driver of that bus chased her—

dirty coat, two puffy eyes—
like any orphan, she refused to cry
as he held her up against that door
till the authorities arrived: one hand

a fist around her shoulder, the other
fingers trembling in her hair.
He wanted to kill her, little piece
of shit, he loved her, little sparrow.

Why did you make me almost kill you?
He said this of course in German:
I could not have understood.
In Michigan a man came home to his

house on a quiet street and found
his son and young wife dead.
The neighbors said he ran outside
and buried his face in damp leaves.

IV. ORIGINS

Darwin only said that change must be
incremental, copious, and undirected.
It was someone else who said the flight
of birds is a fortunate consequence.

I think often of that ink traced
invisibly in our minds, indelible memory
that speaks of other origins, histories
about which we seem only to possess

the dimmest notion. What was it that you said
to me that night down by the river?
Perhaps that I reminded you of those
endangered cranes returned now to the marsh.

I would, of course, misunderstand
with your hand on my throat like that—
believing you thought me beautiful
and rare: already wounded and the hunters'

boots advancing through the sumac.
But later you would ask me how
I dared presume that all your words
were there for taking—like those cranes

glutted on farmers' grain: a dim memory
of ravaged fields, the moon always
beckoning from the marsh's edge.
Darwin waited years to tell his story,

fearing he would be misunderstood.
Anyway, this is the myth. Among
the scholars there is some contention
on this point. We know that he

filled notebooks endlessly revising
metaphors: *war of nature,*
battle of nature, struggle of nature....
These incremental changes constituting

something he first noticed in the
movement of a river's stones—
copious and undirected. In truth,
you said nothing about cranes

that night. The story was my own.
You spoke only of another woman
so in love with you she tried to drown
herself. Your words, there for taking.

V. Tattoos

Do our stories ever end? I'm unsure
about the untold ones—half remembered—
that seem to tell themselves again,
again, again. At twenty-one,

our dad came home and gave a girl
a ring another had returned to him.
Our mother told us this in confidence
when we were girls. She said she didn't mind:

the ring so beautiful—the rare setting
of its stones. He never spoke about
the journey of that ring. We knew
we couldn't ask. But secretly we thought

the story of the jilting might be told
in his tattoo. And so we sought for clues
on the front of his right arm: a deep
blue heart, and inside—the flourish

of a name. Once, while he slept, we pushed
away the hairs and tried to read: *Mildred*
or *Madeline*—we couldn't be sure—the years
had blurred the ink. And besides

we feared that arm that swooped so easily
from steering wheel to backseat insolence,
from dinner table to a smart-mouth daughter.
Melvin always got it worse than me

he cried in grief one night when I ran
into the room. It must have been part of
some other older story—about a father drunk,
a leather belt, and not enough to eat.

Uncle Mel's an old man now. So are
all those brothers who left home prepared
for war, their only journey. *It's over now,*
our father says. *We won. And that's all.*

THE LIVING AND THE DEAD

LIFE AFTER

After the doctors have left
the patient rises from the bed
and another woman bends over a brown river
to wash the blood from a shirt
and somewhere a prisoner asks again
for a piece of paper.
This is our life after the diagnosis,
after the names have been released
and the forest of our childhood burned.

Following bursts of lengthy applause
the dictators with shiny faces have sat down.

It is time for counting the living
and the dead, for sending out
a delegation, for drafting the list
of possibilities. It is time
to tell the whole story of what happened.

Someone walks on tubular legs to a window
and looks out at the poisoned world.
The river. The forest. The tricky
languages of blood. It's clear now.
The bones of the wrist are visible
and the curve of the skull.

CYCLOTRON

for Jeannie Marshall

In the dream my job
is to hold you under the cross hairs
of a machine designed to fire
subatomic particles through solid materials.
We are in an underground bunker.
The walls are bare cinder block
on which hang masks shaped like human faces.
The doctors instruct me how to immobilize
you. I part your legs and pin your arms.
It is not clear if I am helping you
or collaborating with them.

In the non-dream my job
is to chat with the radiology
technicians in the Control Room
and watch you on closed-circuit TV
lying under the cross hairs
of a machine designed to fire
subatomic particles though solid materials.
You are in an underground bunker.
The walls, bare cinder block,
are covered with masks used to hold
the faces of those receiving
proton-beam therapy to the head.
I twist my legs around the legs
of a plastic chair and fold my arms.
I am trying to beam a message to you
through the monitor, through the concrete,
through the body cast that holds you.

In the dream something goes wrong
with the equipment. Radiation
leaks out everywhere over both
of us. It feels like the orange light
from subway station heat lamps.
I try to pull you to safety
but we can't move. The doors
lock. Our voices are immobilized
by the blare of emergency sirens.
We are falling down a shaft,
accelerating in a tube.
There is darkness and speed.
There are no station stops.

In the non-dream you get dressed.
We walk on our legs across the Harvard
parking lot. The guard waves good-bye.
Our arms brush snow from the windshield
of your car. We could be
two young professors on our way
to a seminar. We could be
two young mothers going home
to our kids. The snow falls harder.
We don't speak.

IT's True, Isn't It?

Trinity
White Sand

It's true, isn't it?

Fernald
Hanford
Amarillo

All true:

Key Lake
Green Run
Rocky Flats
Yucca Mountain
Oak Ridge
Three Mile
Island

Isn't it?

Isn't it true:

What happened to
the Marshall Islanders.

What happened to
the Lapland reindeer.

What happened to the people of West Africa
who hunted and ate the migrating songbirds
who had flown over a place called

Chernobyl.

DEPARTURE

1.
For days they lifted buckets
of eels from the river. The Rhine.
Das Gift. The eels were dead.
From the papers we copied down numbers:
how many tankerfuls of pesticide
for how many kilometers for how many years.
About this, the old masters have no words
for us. Anger works the poison deeper
and each night the barges went on colliding.
A departure from accepted procedures.

2.
In Minnesota that spring, a woman
spent some days bent to a radio.
She was trying to follow the wind's path
from Kiev. When it passed over Red Wing
the cows' milk swam with cesium.
She was advised not to be concerned.
She climbed the fire tower
and scanned the clouds, watched an eagle
lift from a stand of old white pine.
She said she didn't know what
she was looking for. *An aberration.*

"Cesium 137 has a half life of 30 years."
A freak accident. "Cesium forms strong bonds
and sinks into the earth fractions
of inches per year." *An equipment
breakdown.* "This is how cesium

enters the grass-cow-milk route."
Every effort is made.

3.
We walked along the Rhine every day
for months—past the *Chemische Werke*
and the Schierstein Bridge and down by the house
where Wagner wrote *Der Meistersinger*
but where he never heard any strain of voice
descend the way cesium descends
into the bones of children. Fish ovaries
ringed with pesticide. *Wholly unpredictable.*

That was the day the American newspapers
ran the picture of the Pennsylvania treasurer
at his indictment emptying the barrel
of a gun into his mouth. *A case
of human failure.* In the cafe
by the docks the foreign workers
filed in, filed out. All morning
we turned pages, copied down numbers.
The river's head, the river's mouth.
The eels still rising.

We hoisted crates of bottled water
up the hill, the accepted procedure.
It's true, isn't it?
Every night they open the sluices.

INSCRIPTION IN A BIRTHDAY CARD

Each year his autumn birthday
reminds them of the time.
They use the day to comment on
what crops can yet be salvaged
from the devastated garden.
And it gives them cause
to marvel at the brevity
of summer or to pause
a moment by the sill together
with folded arms and watch
the falling leaves unveil the town.

This morning she took the cookbook down
off its high shelf and shooed him
from the house. She bakes
a different cake each year,
proceeding through the recipes
in order, picking up where she
left off before. The years
aren't as different as the cakes.
All their seasons melted into this one
stout candle he'll blow out
again to make her happy.
"Maggie," he'll say, pushing back
his plate, "each cake is better
than the last." Then he'll unwrap
the annual box and feign surprise to find
a sweater in yet another shade of red.

This year is German honey cake.
"Walter, sometimes I'm afraid
to think of what's ahead.
Sifting flour by the sill I noticed
I could already make out through the elms
the outline of the city hospital.
And Walter, while moving through
this book's thick pages I've realized
there are more cakes than birthdays left,
oh my husband, many more recipes than years."

Lecture for a Large Auditorium

In many people's dreams, they find themselves standing at a podium and they are terrified. Maybe they are naked or have forgotten their notes or people are laughing. They want to run away. As for myself, I flee to podiums. And here is my central point: At a podium, there are people who are watching, people who are listening. Who will listen for up to one hour. Because that is the convention. You can explain anything in an hour.

Moreover, as long as I am talking here, nothing bad can happen. No one will call me into their office and close the door. No one will ask me to suck their dick. No one will inform me there is a shadow on the X-ray. No one will steer me by the elbow and say, "Now, Sandra...." You can be flown to cities you have never seen, picked up by strangers in airports and brought to podiums. You can explain about the 12 million migrating songbirds, about the chromosomes of sea mammals, about carbon dioxide. You can compare the average lifespan of Ethiopian and American farm workers: 46 years and 49 years, respectively.

The police will come later, the doctors will come later, the President of the United States will come later. When you are somewhere else. [Gesture to empty chair on stage.] Maybe there's a knock on the door. Maybe you answer the phone or turn on the TV. They will say, *Sit down.* And then, they will explain things to you. Straighten you out on the issues. They will say things so terrible that you cannot speak. They will show you the reports, which may or may not be true. They will show you pictures in photo albums with captions so you can see what suffering is really like. Away from the podium you will have to face the consequences, you will have to wait.

To conclude: You will be alone. You will have to defend yourself. It will go on far longer than one hour.

FOR STAR, WHO DID NOT PASS BIOLOGY 114

Pinned under this granite paperweight
rests the evidence of your negligence
and xerox copies of my repeated warnings—

> *Star, you are in danger of . . .*
> *Star, please recognize the gravity of . . .*

And here beside your name in my red ledger:
a long row of zeros, blank faces
that will testify to your truancy.
This is the last afternoon of the last day
of the semester and I am tired
and you are in my office for the first time,
blinking incredulously.

During your tearful defense I recall
how you swept into my classroom
last August, dressed in white
and insisting we call you Star
even though my computer roster
had named you a simple Cathy.
Now you are sobbing into your hands
and I am watching my fingers
test the weight of a pencil
and considering how uncomfortable
we both will feel when we meet
by inevitable accident at some later time,
in line at the theater or in a restroom mirror.

After you make your furious exit
I watch from my window as you
teeter down the icy steps
in ridiculous footwear and disappear.
Tomorrow is the year's shortest day.
Somehow I hope against the growing dark
that you will always refuse to hoist
the implements of duty and responsibility.
Star, I had wanted to tell you
how when I married I chose against all advice
to keep my father's unwieldy Germanic name
that means *a digger of stones.*

FUNERAL SERVICE FOR ABBIE HOFFMAN

Prelude
It was and is April 1989.
We were waiting to hear the weather.
That's when the TV news came on and we heard them say
that you were dead, Abbie Hoffman.

Testimonial
I was a child, Abbie, when you went underground. Sitting
in front of the television, I wondered what was it like down
there?
I imagined tunnels lit with bare light bulbs, dripping wa-
ter, stacks of newspapers, and somewhere the sound of a
typewriter. I bet there are a lot of people down there, I
told my sister.
Down there under ground.

Processional
To escape from prison, Cock Robin disguised himself as
his own assassin.
Do you remember the story?
Is that what this is all about?

Burial
This poem is about death and survival and the image of
the underground, which is a metaphor for both.
This poem is not a eulogy.
This poem is not about nostalgia.

This poem despises New Age.
This poem is not about paralysis.
This poem has nothing to do with commitment, diversity, excellence, image enhancement, deniability, institutional strengthening, or the Chronic Fatigue Syndrome.
This poem does not acknowledge deterrence theory, the Gaia Hypothesis, retro-feminism, or the Operation Rescue of the mommy track.

This poem prohibits all stories about democratic elections in Paraguay, white people carved up by voodoo drug dealers, or how much blood spilled out of the body of an investment banker in Central Park.

This poem is about the wind in the garden.
This poem is about scorched earth.

This poem saw a man with a cardboard sign that read "I am homeless, have AIDS and no money. Please help. Proof available."
This poem is about a man with a cardboard sign times 53 thousand already dead, is about 20 million hungry Americans times 80 percent who are women and children, and we're going to sit here until we've said all their names.

This poem is good at math.

This poem is getting angry.
This poem is piecing its weapons together.
This poem is going to rise up out of the underground and seize the means of expression.
This poem is for Abbie Hoffman.
Now, everybody, start singing.

Village Health Care Handbook

Be kind. Do not let anyone tell you
there are things you should not know.

Know your limits—but also use your head.
It helps to keep certain basic questions in mind.

What are the different houses made of?
Is the cooking done on the floor?

How does the smoke get out?
Where do people put their garbage?

Hungry children do not work well
and many of them die.

When people think that someone
is bewitched it is not true

that he will get well
if his relatives kill the witch.

It is true that when the soft spot
on top of a baby's head sinks inward

this means the baby will die
unless it gets special treatment.

Sometimes diseases that have different
causes look very much alike.

Malaria begins suddenly.
Typhoid begins with a cold.

Malta fever begins slowly with tiredness,
headache, and pains in the bones.

This may go on for months
or years.

Many problems can be corrected by digging latrines.
No one is ever helped by harming someone else.

Do not let pigs come into your house.
Do not spit on the floor.

Do not eat food that is old or smells bad.
Be careful with canned fish.

Sometimes a tea made from corn silk
can help reduce swelling of the feet.

Boil a large handful in water and drink
one or two glasses. It is not dangerous.

Try to do no harm.
Remember it is easy to make mistakes.

When you send someone for help always send
a completed information form.

Never send a small child or a fool.

LuAnn

for LuAnn Keener

1.
What I remember most is how you couldn't
sleep, the missiles lobbing again, again
into Arkansas, the way they really did.

In your dreams the people leapt from
collapsing bridges, bodies streaming
toward the river for salvation as something

white disappears behind the trees.
It kept you stationed at our window,
building words to stop the bombs.

In your poems the barbed wire rolls
in tides around the forests,
the camps, the orchards where a girl

holding fruit sees her mother
gunned into the dust. She will live,
you said, and learn to speak.

2.
Driving north, I think of your insistence.
Already in the fields the wild carrot
has curled its petals into fists of seed.

Or call it Queen Anne's Lace,
it doesn't matter. What's essential
is to learn to tell this flower

from the deadly water hemlock
blooming by the river. The names
are less important than I thought.

You taught me this: When we say
we smell rain we mean that
we smell dust or metal.

3.
What's essential we must rescue.
When the plea of the man whose arteries
had failed him reached the mother
of the brain-dead youth, for a single moment
it all came down to someone running—
disheveled and in tennis shoes—

from a helicopter across a hospital roof
holding out a box packed with ice
and a human heart. Or when

the journalists were mowed into
the streets of Bangkok, how
one camera's eye kept on recording

in the cameraman's dead hand, and saw
the wounded body of his friend,
the soundman, carried off to safety.

We suffer so many emergencies.
The coup failed. The prince
was touring Rome. Only hours later

the soundman also died.
But I am trying to believe
there is a man lying in that hospital

still astonished at the sound
his chest makes. You said it first:
so much depends upon our courage

to invent the gestures of survival.
Yes, it's true. The coup failed,
the insurgents were disposed of.

But then what? *Then what?*
Then there must have been a person
standing in a darkroom trying

to control the tremor in her hand,
having just learned what she has saved.
Can you hear her whisper to herself,

My God, it's all here on film.

4.
The pages of your poems lie in my lap
while I am writing. This is the story of
two girls in Arkansas who learn to walk

the corridors between the trees. Perhaps
it smells like rain. Perhaps the woods
are full of bombs and shallow graves.

Soon they'll find a river where
the summer twilight folds itself
into the water like a cloth,

and one of them will gesture
toward a bridge from which—look—
no one is leaping.

LuAnn, do you see it, how strong
those girders are where I have blow-torched
the letters of your name?

FIELD

Disappearance is death's smallest brother.

Anuak proverb

1.

October tilts into darkness.
Something clarifies:
an axis, a disturbance.
By a north window in north country
I am reading about whorls
on the thumbs of peasants.
Glass ballot boxes. Indelible
stamps in the passbook.
There is nothing to hold the light
as it flees from this room.
As elsewhere, the soul itself
flees from the hacked body
into darkness.

2.

There is the dream of the field.
There is the dream of fire.
There is the dream of the field, fire,
many bodies running.

3.

I said: *There are places where the bodies*
              lie in the open fields like fruit.
              I have seen them.

You said: *There are places where the bodies*
              disappear before they even fall.

4.
A chalice tilts in California.
After twenty years of fasting
Cesar Chavez is breaking bread
at High Mass. Across the red fields
his sons steer him to the altar, his body
transparent as a glass ballot box.

5.
You said: *Here is such a place.*

6.
Field of vision
Field of knowledge
Field of battle
Field of influence
Field of tomatoes

7.
Now they are gathering the glass boxes.

Deep in the jelly of the eye,
deep in the mirrors of the camera,
something is moving. A light is fleeing.

8.
Another disturbance in the bloody fields.

9.
This is October, the final plebiscite.
In the north room of a courthouse
in my own country the defendants
file in. Whatever they say to you
say nothing.

10.
We saw the doctors talking
with the police. We saw
all you fuckers out in the fields
disappearing the bodies,
driving those trucks of fruit
down that road.

GROUNDWATER

for E. Susan Burt (1937-1989)

Why your picture in the morning paper surprises me I
don't know. I was the one who drove from the hospital to
your mother's house, let myself in with a borrowed key,
rummaged through the figurines and plants and china cups
like a thief until I found the family album. I was the one
who turned each plastic-coated page. I was the one who
noticed there were no pictures of you by yourself, how
you positioned yourself in the middle of the rest of us, as
if you had planned to stay with the living always, how
impossible you made this choosing.

And I was the one who said, "Here is one that might work."
Your son sat next to me on the couch. "They'll have to
crop it. What do you think?" Whatever he said was inau-
dible. And I was the one who peeled that photograph from
the gummy adhesive, aware that the dead are always culled
from the living like this. And I was the one who handed
the picture to the funeral director. Someone else correctly
spelled the names of the survivors. That was last night.

This morning—as though night and day were any differ-
ent—you are the one who smiles alone above your obitu-
ary, and I, who saw the sun rise five times from your hos-
pital window, am surprised. I buy a second copy of the
newspaper, and then a third. I want to buy all the copies
of the newspaper, but I know you are already lying on a
thousand porches, stacked beside a thousand counters,
locked inside a thousand metal boxes that even now the
coins are dropping into.

You are the one who taught me that an aspirin added to the water of cut flowers will preserve them. I have done this now for years.

Smash the vase named Survivor. Let the funereal flowers be flung from the water. Let the half-dissolved tablet eat a hole in the floorboard. As the dead evaporate, the living behave like water. We want to fall. We want to run through gullies to the bottom lands, mingle with dirt, lie down with roots and worms, turn paper back to pulp, leach through rocks, be pulled underground.

Under the earth, a thousand rivers flow. On the far banks, the dead are massing, wrapped in white hospital blankets, waving arms encircled with plastic name tags, their faces unsurprised, indivisible.

Outpatient

Once again I dress in white
paper and climb onto the table.

Oh, I can be as gallant about this
as anyone.

The paper is meant to amplify
the bristle of body hair
and breathing. Its whiteness
illuminates the blue-green net
cast just below the skin.
The way it crumples and soaks through
is to remind the wearer of the body's
humidity. I am usually allowed
plenty of time to sit like this alone
in a current of too-cool air.
The doorknob admires my stillness.
The stirrups regard me blandly.
Stainless, I say. *Let me be
as stainless as you.*
In another room, my street clothes
wait loyally, bundled in their cuffs,
their casings, arm holes, leg holes,
still warm to the touch.
In another room, beneath the big TV,
you must be waiting too.

Can the world, if it loves us,
bind us here? Yesterday, the weather
was unseasonably warm. We walked
along the lake out to the bike shop.
You showed me the expensive pedals
that you won't allow yourself to buy.
Still, you laid them in my hands
and had me test the heft of them.
They were airy, cool, perfect.
You spoke rhapsodically on form
and function, on the virtues of forged
steel and anodized aluminum. Titanium
gives lightness. The cam is what
connects the cycle to the rider's shoe.
The finest ones release at 22 degrees.
I believed you deeply.
Yesterday, I unsutured the dog,
already healed from the operation
she seems to remember nothing of.
You held her body. I pulled
the black threads deftly
through the shaved belly skin
and assured you both that I was fitted
for this work by years of practice.
I once transplanted the limb bud
of a chick embryo *in vivo,*
a clean job—the professor praised it—
not to mention all the fetal pigs
and sharks and sheep hearts.
I think you were impressed.
The dog lay calmly in your hands
and watched me. *I will live*
as long as you, I swore to her.

Out in the hospital parking lot,
honeysuckle buds break dormancy by virtue
of an elaborate chemical pathway.
I choose a favorite ceiling tile
and smooth my paper gown.
The doorknob turns, compressing
a spring that retracts
a bolt from a perfectly
aligned space in the wall

and I am ready.

ENVOI: DISBANDING THE ANGELS

Some are resplendent, iridescent,
bowed heads and oiled hair.
Others: armed thugs
in mirror shades. Nights

when rage (or fear) descended
like a flock of birds,
days when the hypodermic needle
skimmed under the skin of my arm

(and we are under the buzzing lights
gliding down the corridor very fast)
I gave orders and positioned
the angels.

I'm returning to civilian life.
You can go home now.
Thanks for your help.

Notes

"Response to a Promotional Ad"

The American Cancer Society's ad no. 0785 depicts a city skyline under a waxing moon together with the message, "More people have survived cancer than now live in the City of Los Angeles. We are winning."

The Grand Calumet flows through northern Indiana. Contaminated with mercury, arsenic, cyanide, chromium, PCBs, oil, phenols, zinc, cadmium, lead, and copper, it is considered one of the most polluted rivers on earth.

Between 1951 and 1963, more than 100 nuclear bombs were exploded in the atmosphere at the Nevada Test Site. More than 700 nuclear bombs have also been detonated underground.

Oak Ridge, Tennessee is the once-secret atomic city constructed by the U.S. government in 1942 to enrich uranium for nuclear weapons. Thousands of pounds of uranium, mercury, and cesium have been released from Oak Ridge into the surrounding air, soil, and water. It remains a contaminated site.

"Bone Scan"

A bone scan is a method of imaging the skeleton. A bone-seeking radioactive isotope is injected into the bloodstream and is absorbed over a two-hour period. The patient then lies motionless on a scanner table while her bones emit gamma rays that expose a plate of photographic film.

"Letter to the City"

The epigraph is from *The Natural History of Deer* by Rory Putnam (Ithaca, NY: Cornell University Press, 1988), p. 61.

"How Are You? Are You Fine?"

The title of this poem comes from an editorial by comedy writer and cancer patient Marilyn Suzanne Miller: "Some people have actually started conversations with me about my health like that: 'So how are you? Fine?'" ("Cancer for Christmas," *New York Times*, December 12, 1992).

"History of Atomic Bomb Testing"

The epigraph is from "Memory Exercises" in *A Little Course in Dreams* by Robert Bosnak (Boston: Shambhala Press, 1988).

Able, Baker, Charlie, Dog...X-ray, Yoke, Zebra are the code words of the U.S. military alphabet as used by radio operators in World War II. Atomic bomb testing began on the Bikini atoll on July 1, 1946 with the detonation of two bombs named Able and Baker.

How Hour refers to the moment a bomb is released from an airplane.

Sidewinder, Redwing, Sandstone, Schooner, Buggy, Sulky, Teapot, Upshot, Bravo, Hardtack, Wigwam, Yucca, and Swordfish are names of atomic bombs or atomic bomb operations.

The debate over the christening of the bikini bathing suit is summarized by Jonathan Weisgall in *Operation Crossroads: The Atomic Tests at Bikini Atoll* (Annapolis, MD: Navy Institute Press, 1994), pp. 263-265.

Zeropoint refers to the end of a countdown.

Operation Crossroads was the code name of the Able and Baker bombings at Bikini.

The diary of Crossroads veteran David Bradley (*No Place to Hide: 1946/1984,* Hanover, NH: University Press of New England, 1983) served as a source for this poem, as did the work of photographers Carole Gallagher (*American Ground Zero,* Cambridge, MA: MIT Press, 1993), Peter Goin (*Nuclear Landscapes,* Baltimore: Johns Hopkins University Press, 1991), and Jim Lerager (*In the Shadow of the Cloud: Photographs and Histories of America's Atomic Veterans,* Golden, CO: Fulcrum, 1988).

Several lines in this poem are adapted from Jeremy Taylor's *Dream Work* (New York: Paulist Press, 1983): "This technique requires you recall your whole waking day, backward, as your last act before going to sleep. You lie in your sleeping place and say to yourself, 'Here I am lying down...here I am changing into my nightclothes...here I am brushing my teeth....' Then in the morning when you first awaken, you repeat the process, only this time it is the night's sleep that is reviewed backward: 'Here I am waking up, here I am asleep having a dream, here is the dream'" (pp. 24-25).

"Research Notes"

The text of part one is based on J.B. Overmier and M.E. Seligman's "Effects of inescapable shock upon subsequent escape and avoidance responding," *Journal of Comparative Physiological Psychology* 63 (1967): 28-33.

The text of part two is appropriated from my pathology reports, doctors' notes, and medical records.

The text of part three is based on various textbook descriptions of infant behavior.

"Apology to Audre Lorde, Never Sent"

"I memorized your words": The quote by Audre Lorde is from *The Cancer Journals* (San Francisco: Spinsters/Aunt Lute, 1980), p. 75. Lorde died of breast cancer in November 1992.

The Huron River runs by the University of Michigan Hospital in Ann Arbor.

"Custody"

The epigraph is from Robinson Jeffers' adaptation of Euripides' *Medea* (New York: Random House, 1946), pp. 100-101.

"Better to be clean bones on the shore...": Act I, p. 42.

"Stories from Memory"

The epigraph by James Agee is from *Let Us Now Praise Famous Men* (Boston: Houghton Mifflin Co., 1939), p. 415.

"Her secret rehabilitation" refers to an arm exercise called the "spider walk" routinely prescribed to women who had undergone Halsted radical mastectomies. Invented by U.S. surgeon William S. Halsted, this surgery involved removing the pectoral muscles as well as the breast itself, leaving women with a sunken chest and weakened arm. The Halsted radical was phased out in 1979.

"Cyclotron"

A cyclotron is a nuclear particle accelerator. The original cyclotron at Harvard University was dismantled in 1943 and moved to Los Alamos, New Mexico, where it played a role in the building of the atomic bomb. Rebuilt in 1948 for the purpose of "contributing to development of atomic energy and the security of the United States," the Harvard Cyclotron Laboratory is located at 44 Oxford Street in Cambridge. Treating cancer patients with inoperable tumors of the eye, spine, and brain became an additional function of the laboratory in 1961.

"It's True, Isn't It?"

Trinity is the name of the first atomic bomb explosion on earth, which took place on July 16, 1945 at the White Sands Proving Ground in New Mexico. Several acres of desert sand were fused into glass.

The Fernald nuclear facility in Ohio produces uranium rods and ingots for atomic weapons. Since 1951, at least 200 tons of uranium dust were intentionally released into the air and water around the facility. The site remains highly contaminated. Fernald is also the name of a school for the mentally retarded in Waltham, Massachusetts. As part of a human experiment begun in 1949, children at Fernald were fed trace amounts of radioactive materials in their breakfast cereal and were told they were joining a "science club."

The Hanford Nuclear Reservation in Washington State transformed uranium into weapons-grade plutonium from 1943 until 1987 and steadily released radioactive materials into the air, soil, and water of the Columbia River. The site remains heavily contaminated.

The U.S. nuclear weapons final-assembly plant—now a bomb disassembly plant and plutonium storage facility—is located in Amarillo, Texas.

Key Lake is the name of a uranium mine in northern Saskatchewan.

Green Run is the name of an experiment conducted at Hanford on December 2, 1949 in which large amounts of radioactive iodine were released into the air, irradiating thousands of downwind residents.

The Rocky Flats nuclear bomb factory near Denver, Colorado has polluted the air, soil, and water with plutonium. Plutonium has a half-life of 24,000 years.

Yucca Mountain in southern Nevada is currently being excavated for consideration as the final burial site for 77,000 tons of nuclear waste.

Oak Ridge provided uranium for the Hiroshima bomb.

The Three Mile Island nuclear power plant near Harrisburg, Pennsylvania experienced a near meltdown on March 28, 1979 and released a plume of radioactive gases into the air. Radioactive water from clean-up efforts was later dumped into the Susquehanna River.

"Departure"

In November 1986, a fire in a chemical warehouse in Switzerland led to the dumping of 66,000 pounds of pesticides into the Rhine River. Under the cover of panic and confusion, other companies released toxic substances farther downstream. A series of mysterious shipping accidents caused the dumping of additional hazardous chemicals into the river.

In April 1986, fallout from the world's first nuclear power plant explosion in the Ukrainian atomic settlement of Chernobyl covered much of Germany with a cloud of radioactive fission products such as cesium 137.

Quoted and italicized phrases are appropriated from editorials and magazine articles about Chernobyl.

Das Gift (German): "poison."

"The wind's path from Kiev" refers to the fall-out contaminated wind from the Chernobyl nuclear accident.

Red Wing refers to the town of Red Wing, Minnesota.

Chemische Werke (German): "chemical factories."

"Funeral Service for Abbie Hoffman"

Political activist Abbie Hoffman (1936-1989) became a fugitive in 1974.

"The story of Cock Robin" is as told by W.D. Snodgrass in *The Death of Cock Robin* (Cranbury, NJ: University of Delaware Press, 1987).

Statistics cited are as of April 1989.

"Village Health Care Handbook"

This is a found poem. The text is from *Where There is No Doctor: A Village Health Care Handbook* by David Werner (Palo Alto, CA: Hesperian Foundation, 1977).

"LuAnn"

On September 19, 1980, a nuclear missile was accidentally catapulted from its silo in Damascus, Arkansas into a wooded area nearby. The warhead did not explode.

"Field"

The Anuak people live along the Gilo and Baro rivers in the Gambella province of Ethiopia.

Cesar Chavez (1927-1993) was the founder and leader of the United Farm Workers union. In 1988, Chavez nearly died after a 36-day fast to protest the spraying of cancer-causing pesticides in grape vineyards.

Lynn Sharon Schwartz's novel, *Disturbances in the Field* (NY: Bantam, 1985) was a source for this poem.

I thank my research assistants Rebecca Braun and Amy Stevens for helping me compile this documentation, and the Radcliffe Research Partnership Program for sponsoring their work with me.

Other titles from Firebrand Books include:

Artemis In Echo Park, Poetry by Eloise Klein Healy/$8.95
Before Our Eyes, A Novel by Joan Alden/$8.95
Beneath My Heart, Poetry by Janice Gould/$8.95
The Big Mama Stories by Shay Youngblood/$8.95
The Black Back-Ups, Poetry by Kate Rushin/$8.95
A Burst Of Light, Essays by Audre Lorde/$8.95
Cecile, Stories by Ruthann Robson/$8.95
Crime Against Nature, Poetry by Minnie Bruce Pratt/$8.95
Diamonds Are A Dyke's Best Friend by Yvonne Zipter/$9.95
Dykes To Watch Out For, Cartoons by Alison Bechdel/$8.95
Dykes To Watch Out For: The Sequel, Cartoons by Alison Bechdel/$9.95
Eight Bullets by Claudia Brenner with Hannah Ashley/$12.95
Exile In The Promised Land, A Memoir by Marcia Freedman/$8.95
Experimental Love, Poetry by Cheryl Clarke/$8.95
Eye Of A Hurricane, Stories by Ruthann Robson/$8.95
The Fires Of Bride, A Novel by Ellen Galford/$8.95
Food & Spirits, Stories by Beth Brant *(Degonwadonti)*/$8.95
Forty-Three Septembers, Essays by Jewelle Gomez/$10.95
Free Ride, A Novel by Marilyn Gayle/$9.95
A Gathering Of Spirit, A Collection by North American Indian Women
    edited by Beth Brant *(Degonwadonti)*/$10.95
Getting Home Alive by Aurora Levins Morales and Rosario Morales/$9.95
The Gilda Stories, A Novel by Jewelle Gomez/$10.95
Good Enough To Eat, A Novel by Lesléa Newman/$10.95
Humid Pitch, Narrative Poetry by Cheryl Clarke/$8.95
Jewish Women's Call For Peace edited by Rita Falbel, Irena Klepfisz, and
    Donna Nevel/$4.95
Jonestown & Other Madness, Poetry by Pat Parker/$7.95
Just Say Yes, A Novel by Judith McDaniel/$9.95
The Land Of Look Behind, Prose and Poetry by Michelle Cliff/$8.95
Legal Tender, A Mystery by Marion Foster/$9.95
Lesbian (Out)law, Survival Under the Rule of Law by Ruthann Robson/$9.95
A Letter To Harvey Milk, Short Stories by Lesléa Newman/$9.95
Letting In The Night, A Novel by Joan Lindau/$8.95
Living As A Lesbian, Poetry by Cheryl Clarke/$7.95
Metamorphosis, Reflections on Recovery by Judith McDaniel/$7.95
Mohawk Trail by Beth Brant *(Degonwadonti)*/$7.95
Moll Cutpurse, A Novel by Ellen Galford/$7.95
The Monarchs Are Flying, A Novel by Marion Foster/$8.95
More Dykes To Watch Out For, Cartoons by Alison Bechdel/$7.95
Movement In Black, Poetry by Pat Parker/$8.95
My Mama's Dead Squirrel, Lesbian Essays on Southern Culture by Mab Segrest/$9.95
New, Improved! Dykes To Watch Out For, Cartoons by Alison Bechdel/$8.95

Normal Sex by Linda Smukler/$8.95

Now Poof She Is Gone, Poetry by Wendy Rose/$8.95

The Other Sappho, A Novel by Ellen Frye/$8.95

Out In The World, International Lesbian Organizing by Shelley Anderson/$4.95

Politics Of The Heart, A Lesbian Parenting Anthology edited by Sandra Pollack and Jeanne Vaughn/$12.95

Presenting. . .Sister NoBlues by Hattie Gossett/$8.95

Rebellion, Essays 1980–1991 by Minnie Bruce Pratt/$10.95

Restoring The Color Of Roses by Barrie Jean Borich/$9.95

A Restricted Country by Joan Nestle/$9.95

Running Fiercely Toward A High Thin Sound, A Novel by Judith Katz/$9.95

Sacred Space by Geraldine Hatch Hanon/$9.95

Sanctuary, A Journey by Judith McDaniel/$7.95

Sans Souci, And Other Stories by Dionne Brand/$8.95

Scuttlebutt, A Novel by Jana Williams/$8.95

S/he by Minnie Bruce Pratt/$10.95

Shoulders, A Novel by Georgia Cotrell/$9.95

Simple Songs, Stories by Vickie Sears/$8.95

Sister Safety Pin, A Novel by Lorrie Sprecher/$9.95

Skin: Talking About Sex, Class & Literature by Dorothy Allison/$13.95

Spawn Of Dykes To Watch Out For, Cartoons by Alison Bechdel/$9.95

Speaking Dreams, Science Fiction by Severna Park/$9.95

Stardust Bound, A Novel by Karen Cadora/$8.95

Staying The Distance, A Novel by Franci McMahon/$9.95

Stone Butch Blues, A Novel by Leslie Feinberg/$10.95

The Sun Is Not Merciful, Short Stories by Anna Lee Walters/$8.95

Talking Indian, Reflections on Survival and Writing by Anna Lee Walters/$10.95

Tender Warriors, A Novel by Rachel Guido deVries/$8.95

This Is About Incest by Margaret Randall/$8.95

The Threshing Floor, Short Stories by Barbara Burford/$7.95

Trash, Stories by Dorothy Allison/$9.95

We Say We Love Each Other, Poetry by Minnie Bruce Pratt/$8.95

The Women Who Hate Me, Poetry by Dorothy Allison/$8.95

Words To The Wise, A Writer's Guide to Feminist and Lesbian Periodicals & Publishers by Andrea Fleck Clardy/$5.95

The Worry Girl, Stories from a Childhood by Andrea Freud Loewenstein/$8.95

Yours In Struggle, Three Feminist Perspectives on Anti-Semitism and Racism by Elly Bulkin, Minnie Bruce Pratt, and Barbara Smith/ $9.95

You can buy Firebrand titles at your bookstore, or order them directly from the publisher (141 The Commons, Ithaca, New York 14850, 607-272-0000). Please include $3.00 shipping for the first book and $.50 for each additional book.

A free catalog is available on request.